James S Foubister IV

This Book Presented

To: _____

From:_____

Occasion:_____

Date: _____

Jesus Reigns In Me

Lord I pray you give me your eyes, so I may
SEE as you SEE

Lord I pray you give me your ears, so I may
LISTEN as you LISTEN

Lord I pray you give me your hands, so I may
SERVE as you SERVE

Lord I pray you give me your heart, so I may
LOVE as you LOVE

Lord I pray you give me your feet, so I may
WALK as you WALK

Lord I pray you give me your mind, so I may be
WISE as you are WISE

Lord I pray you give me your armor, so I may be
COURAGEOUS as you are COURAGEOUS

Lord I pray you give me your humility, so I may
PRAY as you PRAY

TABLE OF CONTENTS

Welcome   viii

1   What is Legacy 31?   Pg 12

2   Are You Ready?   Pg 31

Legacy 31 Days

1   Commandments   Pg 43

2   Conviction/Attitude   Pg 48

3   Encouragement   Pg 53

4   Prayer   Pg 58

5   Faith/Hope   Pg 62

6   Finance/Tithing   Pg 66

7   Forgiveness   Pg 70

8   Mercy   Pg 74

9   Gossip/Tongue   Pg 78

10 Grace   Pg 82

11 Heart   Pg 87

12 Heaven   Pg 91

13 Humility/Pride   Pg 95

14 Integrity/Reputation   Pg 99

Treasure In Heaven   Pg 103

15 Kindness   Pg 107

16 Love   Pg 111

17 Loyalty   Pg 115

18 Marriage/Family   Pg 119

19 Missions   Pg 123

20 Motives/Truth   Pg 127

21 Pastors   Pg 131

22 Eternity   Pg 135

23 Priorities   Pg 139

24 Purpose for Christ   Pg 143

25 Reading Scripture   Pg 147

26 Salvation   Pg 151

27 Serving Others   Pg 155

28 Sin   Pg 159

29 Trinity   Pg 163

30 Unity   Pg 168

31 Wisdom   Pg 172

32 Your Day   Pg 178

Well Done   Pg 179

Legacy 31

Welcome

Thank you for providing your descendants a picture of your life, heart and motives for Jesus Christ.

As we begin, please keep in mind that this author is a simple man. The Lord provided me with a heart to accept His call to salvation. It is an honor to have received His offer and then have Christ live in me. I have no formal training in theology or doctrine.

Upon my salvation at age forty-seven (2001), His message to me was one of **UNITY** in Jesus. That there is no denomination in heaven. That all believers of Jesus should come together to love one another and those in need. In that way, the world will see we are his true disciples.

(John 13: 34-35) So now I am giving you a new commandment: Love each other. Just as I have loved you should love each other. Your love for one another will prove to the world that you are my disciples." His gift to us is His promise of eternal life with him forever. We can believe this truth, because God cannot lie. This truth opens our eyes and hearts toward eternity. We all decide what our eternity will be like. After salvation, what we believe eternity will be like determines all our decisions and actions. The more convicted we are that our eternal expectation is real, then the more focused we are in our choices. The less we believe in eternity, the less we decide to be like Christ.

The Lord has made it clear to me that Christian heritage is extremely important as we move into the next two centuries. Not important to you and I but very important to those who follow us.

The Lord's Prevenient Grace

My family moved to Sarasota, Florida, August 1st, 1998 from Winnipeg, Manitoba. August 3, 1998, while driving on Bee Ridge Road in Sarasota my nine year old son, Jimmy, announced he wanted to be baptized! Since I had never been to church I shared with Chris, my wife, that he would forget about it. The next day, Dutch Richardson our realtor and the only person we met in Florida, invited us to church. We accepted the invitation and our life changed forever as we walked through the doors of Sarasota Alliance Church.

Pastor Ron Hiers and his wife, Dawna, welcomed us August, 1998. Pastor Ron interviewed Jimmy and Jimmy had an extraordinary understanding of Jesus, the trinity, salvation and who Jesus was. Jimmy had learned this while attending the Winnipeg Mennonite Elementary School in Winnipeg, MB.

When Jimmy was baptized in October, 1998, my job had me travel 35 weeks a year when we were in Sarasota. So I was of little help encouraging Jimmy and my wife, Chris', walk with Christ in the first two years when we arrived in Florida. My loving wife, Chris, accompanied Jimmy every Sunday and Wednesday at Sarasota Alliance.

I surrendered my life to Christ in December 2001. Fully accepting Jesus as Lord of my life. My wife, Chris insisted we become baptized in October, 2002.

This was the most significant declaration I made and my wife, Chris, was very wise in encouraging me to be baptized. Pastor Ron baptized me at Siesta Key, Florida, and as I rose out of the water, I was truly a new creation and have tried to honor Christ every minute after my baptism.

I do not write this book to boast about what I have done, but what Christ has done in me.

My hope is when my descendants read this they will know the most important thing about my life was, "I loved God with all my heart, all my mind, all my strength and all my soul. And I loved my neighbors as myself"

In one hundred years, they will not need to know my career, net worth, position, hobbies, or possessions. What they need to know, is how they can live with Jesus Christ in eternity! I will be in heaven waiting for them!

Chapter 1

What is Legacy 31?

Legacy 31 is your spiritual gift to your family. It also defines your love of Christ. The 31 days, where you share your life and love of Christ, will provide you with a clear visual of the person you are in Christ. As the name suggests, Legacy is for your family to come to know you now, next year, ten years, fifty years or one hundred years from now. Whenever the Lord opens the door, you can share your Legacy 31, in person or long distance.

Disciple Making

The scripture is clear we are to make disciples. Your Legacy 31 will act as a written witness for people who are seeking Christ's answers in their life. It will be important as the Holy Spirit moves in the people who read your Legacy 31.

This is your 31 day devotional, there are no correct answers or wrong answers. It is sharing what your Holy Spirit is telling you.

Truth Factor in Christ

As you pray for your spiritual faith, be aware that building **your** Legacy 31 could be the most significant 31 days of your spiritual walk. Because You will seek the truth, discover the truth and accept the truth about your faith in Jesus.

This is not a self-improvement exercise or self-motivational game.

It could be the first time in your life you are 100% truthful about your faith in Christ, what scripture defines you, and what verses and beliefs are non- negotiable in your faith.

Where are your truths, your faith center that defines the person you are today? Not the person you were, not the person you want to be, but the person you are now!

Your life and love of Christ is not a competition. It is your heart as it relates to Christ, and we call it faith. The confidence of what we hope for will come true. **Hebrews 11:1** Faith is the confidence that what we hope for will actually happen; it gives us assurance about things we cannot see.

After you complete this assignment, you will be firmly planted in your spiritual walk. Remember there is no correct answer. You do not get the answer sheet.

All you get is you! You will find the entire truth about you, as a person, as a parent, as a grandparent, as a son or daughter, as a spouse, as a friend and as a Christian.

This is indeed a priceless gift if you are to accept it.

Search the scriptures, and record all the verses which define your faith. Place them in the day/topic which best fits your perspective.

Then write the perspective of why this verse is important to you.

Do not ask anyone's opinion; this is between you and Jesus.

You will be stronger for Christ after you have completed Legacy 31. This Legacy will be where you turn when your sinful nature is being tempted, when you are persecuted, when you are down, when you are lost, and when you are not sure. Legacy 31 is your cross and will energize, comfort and direct you the rest of your life.

You may quit this challenge any time in the 31 days!

The truth will set you free, but know the truth may be difficult to accept.

Have you ever thought of your Christian lineage?

You may be the first generation Christian in your family to lead a convicted life for Christ! You could be the second, third or even sixth generation. What could it mean in your walk if you could be inspired by knowing the faith and truth about your parents, grandparents, or great grandparents' faith! What a blessing indeed.

Legacy 31 will offer your unique spiritual life to the next generations the Lord has promised you. They will come to know your heart for Christ. Your Legacy could be a key factor in their salvation and their walk, after you are in heaven!

Perhaps this is exactly what Jesus meant when he said "Pick up your cross and follow me!"

When you know your true cross, you will know the true you.

Christ will always bless and use the truth for his great purpose. He will use truthful people for His mission.

It is helpful to date your Legacy as you build it. As you grow closer to Christ, new verses will be revealed as truth to you and become important. Date and add these verses as soon as the Holy Spirit moves you. You are transforming to be like Christ, so it makes sense that your foundation in faith will grow and evolve as well.

What if the opportunity arises where you can share your Legacy with family before you pass? If this happens, pray for the wisdom to share in a calm, patient, loving and humble spirit.

You know your verses and the whys and whens, they do not. Details are extremely important. So be prepared to move very slowly to ensure your truths are clear to them. Remember this is not a race with them but your chance to deliver a deep spiritual truth to them.

Be on guard as our human nature could entice us to deliver our explanation in a self-important, self-righteous, prideful or successful attitude. This would then work against our witness. Be encouraged that your Holy Spirit will deliver your Legacy truths in a loving, joyful, patient, faithful, good, peaceful, gentle, kind, and self-controlled spirit.

By accepting your true faith in Christ, you can approach and live with God more closely. We can use His great power in our lives for His purposes. God in turn will reveal more truths for us as we live closer to him.

God will affirm the truths we accept about ourselves, blessing us more each day. When our hearts, motive, and character are pure and true, He will use us for His purpose.

Guard that Legacy 31 does not accidentally become a bragging tool. God will give you great wisdom, love and humility to share your faith in an impactful way for him.

To God be the Glory for your convicted love of Christ.

Before you begin to build your Legacy, there are three truths you must believe.

Do you believe in your heart, Jesus was the son of God, came to earth, died for you, was raised from the dead and His blood washed away your sins?

Do you believe the only way to heaven is through Jesus, the Messiah?

Do you believe in the Trinity, the Father, Son and Holy Spirit?

These three truths are the very foundation of your Legacy. These truths will be the firm foundation to build your life and cross. If you have any questions on these truths, stop and immediately see your pastor. Your very salvation is depending on these truths.

Your faith requires diligent bible study and continuous implementation of your faith values every day. Our sinful nature can have us take our faith for granted, believing by mistake that our faith can never grow weak or disappear completely. Faith is not an inanimate object. Faith is a growing, changing spiritual essence in our souls.

Your faith is witnessed hundreds of times a week when your spiritual moments occur. These spiritual moments are your reaction to your thoughts, how you handle a difficult co-worker, client, teacher, student, friend, family member, teammate, neighbor or stranger. These moments can be in person, by phone or email. You experience spiritual moments, every day.

In fact faith is the essential for living with the joy of the Lord. Faith alone fuels our attitude. Your attitude determines your answers, your actions, your decisions, your motives and your choices. We must have the attitude of Christ.

Therefore, your faith in Christ is the defining point of your very existence.

So, build your Legacy joyfully using truth as the main ingredient mixed with a generous portion of love and the elixir of hope.

When your Legacy is completed for the first time, your Lord may call you immediately to new service.

This is the blessing and reward He offers to His followers, whose heart and motives are true and pure.

Ultimately, the Lord offers you an extravagant gift, when he sees a pure heart and mind working in his follower, together for his purpose. This gift Christ gives to a select few is the gift of contentment. You cannot earn this gift He offers. He gives it only to those who come close to him. How close you ask? Close enough that He hands it directly to you. He sees the truths in your life. He sees your heart and motives. He sees you drawing near and He is prepared for you with open arms. His loving Grace is never more evident than when He hands you His gift of contentment. His most treasured gift.

God has no favorites. He does have close friends. I pray you would be His friend!

Watch out for this common mistake. We sometimes think our family will figure it out on their own. Or we pray a Christian person will lead them to understand.

The answer is for you to get involved for them. Do you love them enough to prepare a spiritual Legacy?

Your Legacy will lead and help them wherever they are, or are not, regarding their faith. Whatever their age, whatever their circumstance, your Legacy will help them.

With your help, their faith will be strong enough to carry them through and over temptation, relationships, discouragement, tragedies, finances, health, back sliding and dealing with the world.

Do we hope someone will come into their life and ignite their love of Christ? Yes, but we need to build a foundation upon which this ignition can occur.
Then, with the foundation in place, a pastor, elder, stranger, friend or neighbor can increase their faith.

Encouragement from Dr. Blackaby

My wife, Chris, and I had the rare opportunity to have Dr. Henry Blackaby and his lovely wife, Marilyn, to our home for dinner with friends. It was in this relaxed setting I had the opportunity to ask the man who wrote **Experiencing God** for some clarification. He was asked what key things he felt we needed to focus on as pastors and leaders in our churches. His response was simple and eloquent.

He shared that we need to pray more often with more conviction and expectation. He then shared that scripture holds our answers. In this culture, our hastiness, self-centeredness and distractions have created Christians who are missing the foundation of bible knowledge. Without this knowledge we will miss knowing God and miss His will in our life.

Dr. Blackaby's observations and wisdom are a key value of the Legacy 31. Know the scripture. By understanding God's word we can evaluate where we are in our transformation to be Christ like. There is no easy short cut in knowing who we are in Christ. Study, prayer and meditation are the blueprint.

Prayer

Prayer is the most intimate time we spend with God. The moments we thank Him, appreciate how He is with us and where we go to know His will in our life.

Jesus instructed us to pray the Lord's Prayer. Each line of this prayer is in itself convicting. "Our Father who art in heaven" is clearly the recognition that God is our Father and is in heaven. "May your name be kept Holy". Here we are to be reverent when we speak of God.

"May your kingdom come soon. May your will be done on Earth as it is in heaven". Here we acknowledge His Kingdom can come anytime. May His will be evident on earth.

"Give us today the food we need and forgive us our sins, as we have forgiven those who sin against us". Here we ask for His favor in supplying what we need. We ask to express His grace to others and receive the same grace we offer others.

"And don't let us yield to temptation but rescue us from the evil one". Here we understand that the temptation is from our own desires and we ask for the Lord's wisdom to protect us from following our sinful nature.

Our prayer life is a powerful catalyst in our walk on earth. We have this incredible inventory of miracles and favor which is best sourced when we pray. To release His favor, we need to be pure of heart and motive. As sinners we will experience short comings in our conviction. It is at those times we employ the power of our Legacy 31 to restore the purity of our mind, heart and soul. This allows us to regain the full power of the Holy Spirit in us. Our prayers continually replenish OUR Holy Spirit which we gracefully and humbly share in our walk with those in our life.

Eternity

As we think about Legacy, we think about eternity. Our faith says we will see many of our generations in heaven. May your Legacy 31 be a blessing to those who you meet in heaven.

Scripture

Scripture is the living word of God. He has provided messengers and prophets to share wisdom and love. The scripture is a key building block for your Legacy. Scripture is the fuel for your Holy Spirit.

Heaven is a denomination free zone

Unity in our churches and with other Christians is the goal Jesus shared in **John 17**. May our unity bear witness to the world: that we are sent by Christ. We know heaven will not have denominations. Let us build heaven on earth with our love and unity for one another.

Love

Jesus shared his final command with his disciples at the last supper. (**John 13: 34-35**) As Judas left the room to betray him, Jesus announced to the remaining disciples, may you love one another as I have loved you. Your love for one another will prove to the world you are my disciples.

No Secret Life

Please do not begin this Legacy if you have a secret life or habit you have not repented for. Any action by a person who knowingly is not obeying God will surely result in an advantage for Satan.

Being truthful is a huge weapon God has for inspiring followers. Satan wins when Christians are deceitful. Your honest relationship with Christ will provide a strong and powerful Legacy for Jesus Christ. Living for Christ is our purpose. May you bless Him today, and always, with your actions.

As You Begin

1   Pray each time you write your Legacy.
2   Take your time to contemplate and reflect as you choose your verses. Your first draft may take six weeks, six months or six years. Do not stress on the timing factor. Be yourself.
3   Add or edit the 31 day topics. You will have important thoughts on scripture and living a life for Christ. Make those adjustments so your Legacy reflects you!
4   Christ is counting on you to persevere, by investing, in prayer and sharing your heart.

Structure Versus Creativity

When we are BORN AGAIN, we begin a personal relationship with Jesus Christ. Legacy 31 has been designed so people can get to know Jesus better. While doing so, they reflect and share all their life, experiences and memories through their perspective.

Personal Devotional

To do this, we need a beginning point, hence the 31 days. This then becomes a personal devotion which is often reviewed. A devotional our descendants and loved ones can enjoy.

The topics, for each day, have been chosen by me from my experiences. Your creativity and story blossoms when you add more days. The book acts as a GUIDE and encouragement to you! What you share is all you!

Form versus Content

The steps I recommend are exactly that, a recommendation. As I completed my Legacy 31, I reflected on key things and the steps which worked best for me. It is the content of what you share, which is ultimately a gift to Jesus Christ and your loved ones. There are many ways to complete your Legacy. What you share is all you!

Design versus Desire

This study is designed for a person to take six weeks of prayerful study and reflection to build the first draft of their Legacy. Our desire is to be truthful and share our deepest emotions and thoughts throughout. This is NOT a race. This is designed to be YOUR ongoing work of worship. The desire is for you to add many times or hundreds of times to this first draft. Your desire will determine the design.

Pride Versus Authenticity

The truth will set you free! The masks we wear in our life are because of mistaken pride. Authenticity is an act of our worship for God. Writing your Legacy could literally remove your masks for the rest of your life. Self-evaluation, which Paul heralds in the scriptures, does not mean to beat yourself up. What he calls us to do is be authentic and truthful.

Completion versus Contemplation

We need to allow ourselves a flexible schedule. Life comes at us very fast from all areas. We need to reflect and pray as we look to begin the challenge of writing a spiritual legacy. Satan may try to convince you that you do not have the talent or the time to write your Legacy. He will try and convince you it does not matter if you write it because no one will read it. That is Satan's lie! God will place your devotional into the hands of people who will love your story. The truth is, Jesus asks us to be available to help make disciples in all nations.

Writing your Legacy is being available. That means you should make the time and take the effort to complete it. Contemplate what success looks like for your Legacy. You are writing this as an act of worship! You are writing this to know Jesus better, to draw close to Jesus, and to share Jesus.

How impactful your devotional will be is unknown now, but, after all, faith is the confidence in what we believe will happen, and the assurance in the things we cannot see.

Chapter 2

Are you ready to start your Legacy 31?

Step 1 It is important to pray before you begin your Legacy 31 journey. Please take some time to prepare your heart and consider the Lord's will for you this month. When you are convicted to share your faith with your future descendants, then you are ready to move on to step 2.

Step 2 Prepare and keep a list of individuals who have encouraged you the most in your walk with Christ. Send a thank you note to one person today.

Example list of individuals who have encouraged me

Let me begin by saying I am always encouraged in some way when I worship and fellowship with believers. **2 Timothy 2:22** "Run from anything that stimulates youthful lusts. Instead, pursue righteous living, faithfulness, love, and peace. Enjoy the companionship of those who call on the Lord with pure hearts." This partial list reflects on how grateful I am for those who love Jesus Christ with a pure heart and invested their time in my life. The Lord has provided me with the opportunity to work with many strong Christian pastors, teachers of the word, and community leaders. This may have continued to your generation as well. It is a gift from God if you are blessed in this way.

Here is a partial list of men who have walked with me for more than 3 years.

One Christ Won City and Friends

Ted Smith, Charlie O'Donnell, Jodey Bruner, Ken
Wagner, Dan Christopherson, Steve Price, Tim
Miller, Jim Foubister Junior, Shannon
Worthington, Matt Koehl, Jon Smith, Kevin
Jessips, Daniels Swanson, Mark Prow, Jeff
Youngberg, Ron Burth, Jack Mya, Joe Ramsey,
Keny Jacobsen, Jack May, George Simbau, Doug
Shamp, Duke Barnes, Tom Mosley, Todd Miller,
Dave Leonhard, Rob Lincoln, Lance Anderson,
Kevin Hander, Howard Flagler, Jim Watt, Mike
Vickers, Butch Terry, Jeffrey Overholt, Billy
Swanson, Ron Perry, Jerry Frimmel, David
Swanson, Bob Kidman, Dean Burnside, John
Rector, Chris Cornette, Isaac Turner, Brian
Wheatley, Craig Faulkner, Jose Valez, Scott Huber,
John Holic, Ed Lavallee, Ed Mogford, Gil Cuadro,
Tony Morley, Gary Crawford, David Russell, Greg
Lee, David Hunihan, Rick Witt, Chuck Denner,
Dale Vollrath, Ken Frailing, Kevin Murphy, Sean
Worthington, Josh Price, Raj Doraisamy, Dutch
Richardson, Rich Sidley, Lee Martin, Earl Carl,
Steve Kennedy, Clint Harris. Bob Fuller, Dennis
Fuller, Dick Armstrong, Wayne Frost, Paul Prachar,
Tom Pfaff, Roger Lee, David Sutton, Jim Clinch,

Jim Ball, JJ Miranda, Lon McCracken, Dave Acker, Bob McBreen, Doc Malwin, Andres Carrero, John Holic, Tom Mattmuller, Larry Menden, Bill Rousseau, Jeff McFarlane, Rick Key.

Pastors

Ron Hiers, Randy Burt, Tom Hodge, Dwight Dolby, Chris Romig, Matt Day, John Meyers, Jim McCleland, Jim MacInnes, Phil Schmunk, Brett Brooks, Jason Bernick, Leon McCrae, Jerry Van Dyken, Jason Warman, Phil Enloe, Bill Philips, Alan Mitchell, Warren Wasson, Paul Warriner, Lawrence Franck, Noel Burke, Stan Farmer, Brian Yost, Kip Hasselbring, Steve Bradshaw, Mike Hudson, Gary Gray, Dale Schlafer, Bob Suter, Steve Rhodes, Bryn MacPhail, Bill Hull, Tony Plummer, Allen Speer, Rabi Simon, Willie Beckham, Jose Ramon Ruiz Perez, Jim Minor, Tom Thies, Rod Myers, Eddie DeJesus, Ramon Cestero, Josh Robinson, Mitch Todd, Rick Shaw, Rod Myers, Rusty Russell, Brian Zdrojowy, Greg Dumas, Guthrie Veetch, Bob Wulvig, Victor Antipov, Vinny Sawyer, Charles Black.

People Who Have Encouraged ME!

_____

_____

_____

_____

_____

_____

_____

_____

_____

_____

_____

_____

_____

_____

_____

_____

_____

_____

_____

_____

_____

Step 3 Write a letter explaining why you are writing this 31 day devotional. Your letter is to your great great grand child, niece or nephew born in (Future date after you are in heaven).

Example Legacy 31 Letter

To a Cherished you,

My prayer and hope for you, is that by spending time in my devotional, you will embrace your spiritual heritage from my life for Christ. As I walked with Christ, into and through many challenges in my life, perhaps in the same way that you have or are experiencing. I wondered about my spiritual heritage.

The spiritual heritage of my ancestors, to me was a gift I wish was available to me. As I believe, with that knowledge, I could have done more for Christ and strengthened my faith.

You have your own relationship with Jesus, which is a gift God sent you. If you have accepted His gift and eternal life, then I say bravo and we will meet in person in heaven.

If you are not sure of your faith in Christ, I say bravo as well. God wants you to repent of sin and accept His son Jesus. God's prevenient grace means He is knocking, at your door today as you read this. If you answer His knock and let him into your heart He sends His advocate, His helper, called the Holy Spirit. (**John 14, 15, & 16**). A life with Christ is a transformation of you, as you know yourself today, into a person the Lord will use to serve and help others experience God's love, through your actions. As you transform, your old wants and desires are replaced by God's wants and the desire to help others.

Time is a fleeting commodity and investing in people with discussions on Christ and building up disciples is a gift the Lord has given to some. Surrounding yourself with people who walk with Christ will strengthen you. You are called to be ready to share your faith with non-believers, not become as they are.

No words can express the love I have for you!
How God, through all the years, has made you
into the man or women, he will use for his
purpose.

Thank you for taking time to spend with me
through this devotion. You cannot change your past
but you can determine your destiny. You cannot
choose your parents, or how big or small you are,
the color of your skin, or what country you are born
in. You alone can choose to embrace and follow
Jesus Christ. My faith is that what I believe will
happen in the future will happen. My prayer is you
will have faith in Jesus Christ, so that one day we
will share together forever, in the Glory of God.

The Lord will never forsake anyone who believes in
their heart and confesses with their mouth that
Jesus Christ is their personal savior. Please reflect
on the encouragement this Legacy 31 is intended to
bring to your heart. Please prepare your own
Legacy 31 and provide your love through a
devotion to those generations who follow you.

My Letter To My Future Descendants

_____

_____

_____

_____

Step 4   Create a personal Mission Statement for your walk with Christ. Two sentence maximum

Example: Let my actions speak of my love for the Lord.

My Mission Statement

_____

_____

_____

Step 5   Complete the 31 day devotional, write the perspective for every day!

Step 6 Remember to revisit your Legacy 31 when the Holy Spirit leads you to. There is space for your future additions to your Legacy. Transformation is a gift God gives you.

"It is cruel to cosign a man to his sin"

-Dietrich Bonheoffer

Day 1 – Commandments

Perspective

When we follow the ten commandments we demonstrate our obedience to God. God's promises for us can only be received as blessings when we are obedient.

Deuteronomy 5

I am the LORD your God, who rescued you from the land of Egypt, the place of your slavery.

You must not have any other god but me

You must not make for yourself an idol of any kind, or an image of anything in the heavens or on the earth or in the sea.

You must not bow down to them or worship them, for I, the LORD your God, am a jealous God who will not tolerate your affection for any other gods. I lay the sins of the parents upon their children; the entire family is affected—even children in the third and fourth generations of those who reject me.

But I lavish unfailing love for a thousand generations on those who love me and obey my commands.

You must not misuse the name of the LORD your God. The LORD will not let you go unpunished if you misuse his name.

Observe the Sabbath day by keeping it holy, as the LORD your God has commanded you.

Honor your father and mother, as the
LORD your God commanded you. Then you will
live a long, full life in the land the LORD your God
is giving you.

You must not murder.

You must not commit adultery.

You must not steal.

You must not testify falsely against your neighbor.

You must not covet your neighbor's wife. You must
not covet your neighbor's house or land, male or
female servant, ox or donkey, or anything else that
belongs to your neighbor.

John 13:34-35

So now I am giving you a new commandment.
Love each other as I have loved you, you should
love each other. Your Love for one another will
prove to the world you are my disciples.

Please Pray Before You Begin

Date:_____

My Key Verses For: Commandments

_____

_____

_____

_____

_____

_____

_____

My Perspective

_____

_____

_____

_____

_____

_____

_____

_____

_____

Please Pray Before You Begin

Date:_____

My Key Verses For: Commandments

_____

_____

_____

_____

_____

_____

_____

My Perspective

_____

_____

_____

_____

_____

_____

_____

_____

''You cannot change your past, but you can determine your destiny''

-Billy Graham

Day 2 – Conviction / Attitude

Perspective

As our life is centered on Christ, we are convicted to transform from the inside to be like Christ. We need to live compassionate lives with the humble spirit as Jesus had.

Such as displaying both empathy and appreciation for every man, women and child, showing no judgment, putting our own needs by the side and honoring others, working together in Christ and for Christ.

Philippians 2:2-5

Then make me truly happy by agreeing wholeheartedly with each other, loving one another, and working together with one mind and purpose.

Don't be selfish; don't try to impress others. Be humble, thinking of others as better than yourselves.

Don't look out only for your own interests, but take an interest in others, too.

You must have the same attitude that Christ Jesus had.

1 Peter 3:8

Finally, all of you should be of one mind. Sympathize with each other. Love each other as brothers and sisters. Be tenderhearted and keep a humble attitude.

Proverbs 2:6-9

For the LORD grants wisdom! From his mouth come knowledge and understanding.

He grants a treasure of common sense to the honest. He is a shield to those who walk with integrity.

He guards the paths of the just and protects those who are faithful to him.

Then you will understand what is right, just, and fair, and you will find the right way to go.

Please Pray Before You Begin

Date:_____

My Key Verses For: Conviction / Attitude

_____

_____

_____

_____

_____

_____

_____

_____

My Perspective

_____

_____

_____

_____

_____

_____

_____

_____

Please Pray Before You Begin

Date:_____

My Key Verses For: Conviction / Attitude

_____

_____

_____

_____

_____

_____

_____

My Perspective

_____

_____

_____

_____

_____

_____

_____

_____

_____

"You pray to God to fix something in your life, but to God it is not broken"

-Billy Swanson

Day 3 – Encouragement

Perspective

Encourage others through words and deeds. Especially focus your help on timid believers. Care for the weak, and be patient with all. When someone trespasses against you, only react with kindness.
When you are joyful, prayerful and thankful, you will be encouraging everyone you meet.

Respond immediately to your Holy Spirit and test all information with your Spirit ensuring it is good for all. Keep your distance from evil people.

1 Thessalonians 5:14-22

Brothers and sisters, we urge you to warn those who are lazy. Encourage those who are timid. Take tender care of those who are weak. Be patient with everyone.

See that no one pays back evil for evil, but always try to do good to each other and to all people.

Always be joyful. Never stop praying Be thankful in all circumstances, for this is God's will for you who belong to Christ Jesus

Do not stifle the Holy Spirit. Do not scoff at prophecies, but test everything that is said. Hold on to what is good. Stay away from every kind of evil.

Hebrews 10:24

Let us think of ways to motivate one and other to acts of love and good works.

Proverbs 3:3-7

Never let loyalty and kindness leave you! Tie them around your neck as a reminder. Write them deep within your heart. Then you will find favor with both God and people, and you will earn a good reputation.

Trust in the LORD with all your heart; do not depend on your own understanding. Seek His will in all you do, and he will show you which path to take. Don't be impressed with your own wisdom. Instead, fear the LORD and turn away from evil.

1 Thessolonians 5:11

So encourage each other and build each other up, just as you are already doing.

Please Pray Before You Begin

Date:_____

My Key Verses For: Encouragement

_____
_____
_____
_____
_____
_____
_____

My Perspective

_____
_____
_____
_____
_____
_____
_____
_____
_____
_____

Please Pray Before You Begin

Date:_____

My Key Verses For: Encouragement

_____
_____
_____
_____
_____
_____
_____

My Perspective

_____
_____
_____
_____
_____
_____
_____
_____

"Blessed are those with a pure heart, for they will see God"

-Jesus Christ

Day 4 – Prayer

Perspective

Prayer is our most powerful gift from God. He provides you a path directly to him. Pray unceasingly with total expectation that God will answer you. Jesus says, pray anything using the name of Jesus Christ and it will be done. When you ask, is your heart pure? Is your motive for God to be glorified?

John 17:8-11

for I have passed on to them the message you gave me. They accepted it and know that I came from you, and they believe you sent me " My prayer is not for the world, but for those you have given me, because they belong to you. All who are mine belong to you, and you have given them to me, so they bring me glory. Now I am departing from the world; they are staying in this world, but I am coming to you. Holy Father, you have given me your name; now protect them by the power of your name so that they will be united just as we are.

Matthew 6:9-15

Pray like this: Our Father in heaven, may your name be kept holy May your Kingdom come soon. May your will be done on earth, as it is in heaven. Give us today the food we need and forgive us our sins, as we have forgiven those who sin against us. And don't let us yield to temptation, but rescue us from the evil one."If you forgive those who sin against you, your heavenly Father will forgive you. But if you refuse to forgive others, your Father will not forgive your sins.

Please Pray Before You Begin

Date:_____

My Key Verses For: Prayer

_____

_____

_____

_____

_____

_____

_____

My Perspective

_____

_____

_____

_____

_____

_____

_____

_____

Please Pray Before You Begin

Date:_____

My Key Verses For: Prayer

_____

_____

_____

_____

_____

_____

_____

My Perspective

_____

_____

_____

_____

_____

_____

_____

_____

"It is not about me, it is not about now!"

-Rick Warren

Day 5– Faith/Hope

Perspective

My faith is what I hope and believe will happen will actually happen. We have confidence and assurance about things we cannot see. Knowing and believing God is with us, and loves us to the end of the age.

Examples of things we cannot not see but we know God is with us and in us are: peace, patience, kindness, gentleness, love, joy, self control, goodness and faithfulness. God has made all things!

Hebrews 11:1-3

Faith is the confidence that what we hope for will actually happen; it gives us assurance about things we cannot see.

Proverbs 5:21-23

For the LORD sees clearly what a man does, examining every path he takes.

An evil man is held captive by his own sins; they are ropes that catch and hold him. He will die for lack of self-control; he will be lost because of his great foolishness.

Jeremiah 29:11-13

For I know the plans I have for you," says the LORD. "They are plans for good and not for disaster, to give you a future and a hope. In those days when you pray I will listen. If you look for me wholeheartedly, you will find me.

Please Pray Before You Begin

Date:_____

My Key Verses For: Faith / Hope

_____
_____
_____
_____
_____
_____
_____

My Perspective

_____
_____
_____
_____
_____
_____
_____
_____
_____

Please Pray Before You Begin

Date:_____

My Key Verses For: Faith / Hope

_____

_____

_____

_____

_____

_____

_____

My Perspective

_____

_____

_____

_____

_____

_____

_____

_____

"An individual has not started living until he can rise above the narrow confines of his concerns to the broader concerns of all humanity"

-Dr. Martin Luther King

Day 6–Finances/Money/Tithing

Perspective

All that we have worked for, and all that has been given to us is from God. We are stewards of the time, talent and treasures He has blessed us with. We are to use what He has provided to glorify Him in faith through deeds. Your generosity with the pure motives places your treasures in heaven. Love and live for Christ and you will have all you need.

Matthew 6:19-21 & 33

"Don't store up treasures here on earth, where moths eat them and rust destroys them, and where thieves break in and steal. Store your treasures in heaven, where moths and rust cannot destroy, and thieves do not break in and steal.

Wherever your treasure is, there the desires of your heart will also be

Seek the Kingdom of God above all else, and live righteously, and he will give you everything you need.

Mark 4:19

But all too quickly the message is crowded out by the worries of this life, the lure of wealth, and the desire for other things, so no fruit is produced.

Please Pray Before You Begin

Date:_____

My Key Verses For: Finances / Money / Tithing

_____

_____

_____

_____

_____

_____

_____

My Perspective

_____

_____

_____

_____

_____

_____

_____

_____

_____

Please Pray Before You Begin

Date:_____

My Key Verses For: Finances/Money/Tithing

_____

_____

_____

_____

_____

_____

_____

My Perspective

_____

_____

_____

_____

_____

_____

_____

_____

"We can stand affliction better than we can prosperity, for in prosperity we forget God"

-D.L. Moody

Day 7 – Forgiveness

Perspective

Jesus teaches us that for us to live as a follower of Christ, we need to first forgive others of their sin, including sin against us. It is us showing grace and mercy which will then provide a path for God to forgive us of our sins.

No matter what our sin is, he will forgive us at our moment of true repentance. God does this immediately and forever.

He provides us a clean spirit every day. How often do we forgive others? Jesus teaches us not 7 times but 7x70. In practical terms forgive everyone always.

Matthew 6:14-15

"If you forgive those who sin against you, your heavenly Father will forgive you

But if you refuse to forgive others, your Father will not forgive your sins.

Matthew 18:21-22

Then Peter came to him and asked, "Lord, how often should I forgive someone who sins against me? Seven times?"

No, not seven times," Jesus replied, "but seventy times seven!

Please Pray Before You Begin

Date:_____

My Key Verses For: Forgiveness

_____

_____

_____

_____

_____

_____

_____

My Perspective

_____

_____

_____

_____

_____

_____

_____

_____

Please Pray Before You Begin

Date:_____

My Key Verses For: Forgiveness

_____

_____

_____

_____

_____

_____

_____

_____

My Perspective

_____

_____

_____

_____

_____

_____

_____

_____

"**God's gift to you each day of mercy and grace is FREE! Share it always with everyone**

-James S Foubister IV

Day 8 – Mercy

Perspective

God's mercy is at the foot of His throne. When we approach Him with faith he will show us mercy as he chooses. He expects us to give mercy to everyone. Especially those who doubt their faith or are seeking him. God's mercy is a gift to us which can only be appreciated when we share mercy with others. Mercy shared is mercy received.

Hebrews 4:16

So let us come boldly to the throne of our gracious God. There we will receive his mercy, and we will find grace to help us when we need it most.

Jude 1:22

And you must show mercy to those whose faith is wavering.

Romans 9:14-16

Are we saying, then, that God was unfair? Of course not!

For God said to Moses, "I will show mercy to anyone I choose, and I will show compassion to anyone I choose."

So it is God who decides to show mercy. We can neither choose it nor work for it

Please Pray Before You Begin

Date:_____

My Key Verses For: Mercy

_____

_____

_____

_____

_____

_____

_____

My Perspective

_____

_____

_____

_____

_____

_____

_____

_____

_____

Please Pray Before You Begin

Date:_____

My Key Verses For: Mercy

_____
_____
_____
_____
_____
_____
_____

My Perspective

_____
_____
_____
_____
_____
_____
_____
_____
_____

"No human being, is conceived outside God's will or ever conceived apart from God's image. Life is a gift from God created in his own image."

-John MacArthur

Day 9 – Gossip/Tongue

Perspective

How you treat gossip will define your integrity & character, which is your true reputation. Yes, the "THINK" filter, before you speak, will save your reputation. Before you speak, see if it fits THINK. Is it? Truthful, Helpful, Important, Needed, Kind!

Stopping gossip from others? If you ARE NOT part of the SOLUTION, stop others from telling you.

If you are the solution and they ask your advice, use scripture to give your answer. You will give an account to God for every idle word you speak. They will acquit or condemn you.

Proverbs 16:28

A troublemaker plants seeds of strife; gossip separates the best of friends.

Proverbs 26:20

Fire goes out without wood, and quarrels disappear when gossip stops

Matthew 12:36-37

And I tell you this, you must give an account on judgment day for every idle word you speak. The words you say will either acquit you or condemn you."

James 3:8

But no one can tame the tongue. It is restless and evil, full of deadly poison.

Please Pray Before You Begin

Date:_____

My Key Verses For: Gossip / Tongue

_____

_____

_____

_____

_____

_____

_____

My Perspective

_____

_____

_____

_____

_____

_____

_____

_____

_____

Please Pray Before You Begin

Date:_____

My Key Verses For: Gossip / Tongue

_____

_____

_____

_____

_____

_____

_____

My Perspective

_____

_____

_____

_____

_____

_____

_____

"Baptism is bowing before the Father and letting Him do His work"

-Max Lucado

Day 10 – Grace

Perspective

Grace is empathy with truthfulness. Christ sent us the Holy Spirit. Not to tolerate or accept sin in people lives, rather to discern the correct scripture which is truth, to share with Love.

This grace brings people with sin, to repent and move closer to Jesus. Our grace will move other people's feelings and needs ahead of our own. Grace is our free gift we give others.

Ephesians 2:4-10

But God is so rich in mercy, and he loved us so much, that even though we were dead because of our sins, he gave us life when he raised Christ from the dead. (It is only by God's grace that you have been saved!) For he raised us from the dead along with Christ and seated us with him in the heavenly realms because we are united with Christ Jesus. So God can point to us in all future ages as examples of the incredible wealth of his grace and kindness toward us, as shown in all he has done for us who are united with Christ Jesus. God saved you by his grace when you believed. And you can't take credit for this; it is a gift from God. Salvation is not a reward for the good things we have done, so none of us can boast about it. For we are God's masterpiece. He has created us anew in Christ Jesus, so we can do the good things he planned for us long ago.

James 4:4-6

You adulterers! Don't you realize that friendship with the world makes you an enemy of God? I say it again: If you want to be a friend of the world, you make yourself an enemy of God

What do you think the Scriptures mean when they say that the spirit God has placed within us is filled with envy?

But he gives us even more grace to stand against such evil desires. As the Scriptures say, "God opposes the proud but favors the humble."

Romans 11:6

And since it is through God's kindness, then it is not by their good works. For in that case, God's grace would not be what it really is—free and undeserved.

Please Pray Before You Begin

Date:_____

My Key Verses For: Grace

_____

_____

_____

_____

_____

_____

_____

My Perspective

_____

_____

_____

_____

_____

_____

_____

Please Pray Before You Begin

Date:_____

My Key Verses For: Grace

_____
_____
_____
_____
_____
_____
_____

My Perspective

_____
_____
_____
_____
_____
_____
_____
_____
_____

"Satan knows your name but calls you by your sin. God knows your sin and calls you by your name!

-James S Foubister IV

Day 11 – Heart

Perspective

Your heart is the TRUE you. What you say reflects the condition of your heart. When the Holy Spirit lives in us our hearts are transformed. We no longer live with pride, selfishness, envy, jealousy, and lust. Transforming, to be like Jesus, is our true heart. Loving others as ourselves becomes our life and the heart of Jesus beats in our chests.

Self-sacrifice, humility, grace and empathy is seen in each beat of our heart. Our eternity is the blood flow to our hearts. When we have pure hearts we will SEE GOD.

Matthew 5:8

God blesses those whose hearts are pure, for they will see God.

Matthew 11:28-30

Then Jesus said, "Come to me, all of you who are weary and carry heavy burdens, and I will give you rest. Take my yoke upon you. Let me teach you, because I am humble and gentle at heart, and you will find rest for your souls. For my yoke is easy to bear, and the burden I give you is light."

Romans 10:9-10

If you confess with your mouth that Jesus is Lord and believe in your heart that God raised him from the dead you will be saved. For it is by believing in your heart that you are made right with God, and it is by confessing with your mouth that you are saved.

Please Pray Before You Begin

Date:_____

My Key Verses For: Heart

_____

_____

_____

_____

_____

_____

_____

My Perspective

_____

_____

_____

_____

_____

_____

_____

_____

Please Pray Before You Begin

Date:_____

My Key Verses For: Heart

_____

_____

_____

_____

_____

_____

_____

My Perspective

_____

_____

_____

_____

_____

_____

_____

_____

"Help someone today. Start with the person nearest you!"

-Mother Teresa

Day 12 – Heaven

Perspective

Heaven is where all followers of Jesus Christ will come together in His presence for eternity. God knows our hearts and motives. He alone, through Jesus Christ, will be our final judge. After that judgment, God will send us to our place in heaven, which He has prepared. There we will celebrate God with other followers forever.

2 Peter 3:13-15

But we are looking forward to the new heavens and new earth he has promised, a world filled with God's righteousness. And so, dear friends, while you are waiting for these things to happen, make every effort to be found living peaceful lives that are pure and blameless in his sight. And remember, our Lord's patience gives people time to be saved. This is what our beloved brother Paul also wrote to you with the wisdom God gave him

Luke 12:33

"Sell your possessions and give to those in need. This will store up treasure for you in heaven! And the purses of heaven never get old or develop holes. Your treasure will be safe; no thief can steal it and no moth can destroy it.

Please Pray Before You Begin

Date:_____

My Key Verses For: Heaven

_____

_____

_____

_____

_____

_____

_____

My Perspective

_____

_____

_____

_____

_____

_____

_____

_____

Please Pray Before You Begin

Date:_____

My Key Verses For: Heaven

_____

_____

_____

_____

_____

_____

_____

My Perspective

_____

_____

_____

_____

_____

_____

_____

_____

"Relationships is the currency of God's Kingdom"

-Will Crooks

Day 13 – Humility/ Pride

Perspective

True humility is present only when your Holy Spirit is in control of your pride. You will have compassion and empathy. The wisdom God teaches you through the scriptures will be evident in your conversation and deeds. Be warned, pride will keep you from the foot of the CROSS and stop you from loving others. Loving others for their gain not yours, is a fine example of humility.

James 3:13

If you are wise and understand God's ways, prove it by living an honorable life, doing good works with the humility that comes from wisdom.

Matthew 5:5

God blesses those who are humble, for they will inherit the whole earth.

Proverbs 11:2

Pride leads to disgrace, but with humility comes wisdom.

Proverbs 22:4

True humility and fear of the LORD lead to riches, honor, and long life.

Please Pray Before You Begin

Date:_____

My Key Verses For: Humility / Pride

_____

_____

_____

_____

_____

_____

_____

My Perspective

_____

_____

_____

_____

_____

_____

_____

_____

_____

Please Pray Before You Begin

Date:_____

My Key Verses For: Humility / Pride

_____
_____
_____
_____
_____
_____
_____

My Perspective

_____
_____
_____
_____
_____
_____
_____
_____
_____

"You need to think more about eternity, not less."

-Rick Warren

Day 14 – Integrity / Reputation

Perspective

Integrity is the measure of one's closeness to God. Good character is when you do the right thing and people see it OR you benefit from that action. Integrity is when you do what is right, just and fair when it is only you and God who will know. Your reputation is impacted the most by how others view your integrity.

Titus 2:7

And you yourself must be an example to them by doing good works of every kind. Let everything you do reflect the integrity and seriousness of your teaching.

Proverbs 10:9

People with integrity walk safely, but those who follow crooked paths will slip and fall.

Proverbs 2:7-9

He grants a treasure of common sense to the honest. He is a shield to those who walk with integrity. He guards the paths of the just and protects those who are faithful to him. Then you will understand what is right, just, and fair, and you will find the right way to go.

1 Peter 2:15

It is God's will that your honorable lives should silence those ignorant people who make foolish accusations against you.

Please Pray Before You Begin

Date:_____

My Key Verses For: Integrity

_____

_____

_____

_____

_____

_____

_____

My Perspective

_____

_____

_____

_____

_____

_____

_____

_____

Please Pray Before You Begin

Date:_____

My Key Verses For: Integrity

_____

_____

_____

_____

_____

_____

My Perspective

_____

_____

_____

_____

_____

_____

_____

_____

Treasures In Heaven

Circles of Saints Who Helped ME

As I share my belief in eternity, do not feel you need to accept such a view. The eternity we believe in is a result of our life with Jesus Christ, our experiences, our memories, our understanding of scripture, and our hope.

I believe that heaven will be a gathering place of all the saints (believers). Saints who preceded us by 1,000 years into heaven and saints who will follow us for 1,000 years. My heaven will have many circles of saints who helped me follow Jesus Christ.

My first circle will be saints who walked with me in my lifetime (mentors and close encouragers) . I do not need to name or identify them, as the Lord knows my heart, and, therefore, will have my mentors and encouragers waiting for me.

My second circle of saints are those who influenced and befriended me. Again, the Lord knows my heart and who will be there.

A third circle of saints are those who prayed with me.

A fourth circle of saints are those who invited me to church.

A fifth circle of saints are those who shared their faith with me.

A sixth circle of saints will be those who showed kindness to me.

A seventh circle of saints will be those who comforted me.

An eighth circle of saints will be those who visited with me.

A ninth circle of saints will be those who worshiped with me.

Circles of Saints Who I Helped

I will receive a much more significant gift from God that He promised me. A **treasure** I stored in heaven while I was here on earth.

On judgment day, as my life and works are passed through eternities furnace, God will reveal to me, in that moment as I enter heaven, his greatest reward for me.

He will place me in the circles of the saints which he sees I deserve. My **treasure,** he promised me in heaven, will be the circles I share as the result of my living a life for him on earth.

I will be in other Saints circles. Those who I walked with in my lifetime (who I mentored and encouraged). I will be in their circle of saints. They do not need to name or identify me, as the Lord knows their heart, he will have me waiting for them.

A second circle of saints are those whom I influenced and befriended. The Lord knows their heart and who I will be there with.

A third circle of people are those I prayed with.

A fourth circle of people are those I invited to church.

A fifth circle of people are those I shared my faith with.

A sixth circle will be those I showed kindness to.

A seventh circle will be those I comforted.

An eighth circle will be those I visited with.

A ninth circle will be those I worshiped with.

My hope is God will find me worthy to place me in many circles.

He knows my heart and motives. Only those works honoring God and doing the work he prepared for me, will be recorded in heaven.

"God has given us two hands, one to receive with and the other to give with."

-Billy Graham

Day 15 –Kindness

Perspective

Kindness is the key to a generous life. Always be willing to provide for others. Empathy is a key virtue you need to have the heart to help others. Random acts of kindness to strangers is the example Jesus gave us. Be kind to everyone, show no favorites, and be willing to help everyone.

Proverbs 11:25

The generous will prosper; those who refresh others will themselves be refreshed.

Colossians 3:12-15

Since God chose you to be the holy people he loves, you must clothe yourselves with tenderhearted mercy, kindness, humility, gentleness, and patience.

Make allowance for each other's faults, and forgive anyone who offends you. Remember, the Lord forgave you, so you must forgive others.

Above all, clothe yourselves with love, which binds us all together in perfect harmony.

And let the peace that comes from Christ rule in your hearts. For as members of one body you are called to live in peace. And always be thankful.

Galatians 6:10

Therefore, whenever we have the opportunity, we should do good to everyone—especially to those in the family of faith

Please Pray Before You Begin

Date:_____

My Key Verses For: Kindness

_____

_____

_____

_____

_____

_____

My Perspective

_____

_____

_____

_____

_____

_____

_____

_____

Please Pray Before You Begin

Date:_____

My Key Verses For: Kindness

_____

_____

_____

_____

_____

_____

_____

My Perspective

_____

_____

_____

_____

_____

_____

_____

_____

_____

"Satan is everywhere you are not supposed to be"

-James S. Foubister IV

Day 16 – Love

Perspective

In the New Living Translation of the bible, there are over two hundred references in the concordance for love. The importance of love will always be understated. Love covers a multitude of sins. Pure love provides you with grace which leads to forgiveness. Love will energize you for doing what is right and just. Jesus teaches us to love God first, and second, love our neighbors.

Mark 12:29-31

Jesus replied, "The most important commandment is this: 'Listen, O Israel! The LORD our God is the one and only LORD. And you must love the LORD your God with all your heart, all your soul, all your mind, and all your strength. The second is equally important: 'Love your neighbor as yourself. No other commandment is greater than these.

1 Corinthians 13:3-7

If I gave everything I have to the poor and even sacrificed my body, I could boast about it, but if I didn't love others, I would have gained nothing. Love is patient and kind. Love is not jealous or boastful or proud or rude. It does not demand its own way. It is not irritable, and it keeps no record of being wronged. It does not rejoice about injustice but rejoices whenever the truth wins out. Love never gives up, never loses faith, is always hopeful, and endures through every circumstance.

Please Pray Before You Begin

Date:_____

My Key Verses For: Love

_____

_____

_____

_____

_____

_____

My Perspective

_____

_____

_____

_____

_____

_____

_____

_____

Please Pray Before You Begin

Date:_____

My Key Verses For: Love

_____
_____
_____
_____
_____
_____
_____

My Perspective

_____
_____
_____
_____
_____
_____
_____
_____
_____

The Great commission is not an option to be considered, it is a command to be obeyed."

-Hudson Taylor

Day17 – Loyalty

Perspective

Loyalty is offering grace to someone in all circumstances. However, it is cruel to show tenderness which cosigns a person to their sin. We need to encourage others with the truth of God's word. Your loyalty is best placed with someone who lives with Christ.

Proverbs 3:3-6

Never let loyalty and kindness leave you! Tie them around your neck as a reminder. Write them deep within your heart. Then you will find favor with both God and people, and you will earn a good reputation. Trust in the LORD with all your heart; do not depend on your own understanding. Seek His will in all you do and he will show you which path to take.

James 5:12

But most of all, my brothers and sisters, never take an oath, by heaven or earth or anything else. Just say a simple yes or no, so that you will not sin and be condemned.

John 14:6

I am the way, the truth, and the life. No one can come to the Father except through me.

Please Pray Before You Begin

Date:_____

My Key Verses For: Loyalty

_____

_____

_____

_____

_____

_____

_____

My Perspective

_____

_____

_____

_____

_____

_____

_____

_____

_____

Please Pray Before You Begin

Date:_____

My Key Verses For: Loyalty

_____

_____

_____

_____

_____

_____

_____

My Perspective

_____

_____

_____

_____

_____

_____

_____

_____

"Followers of Jesus are called to get out of the pews and into the streets to help others!"

-James S Foubister IV

Day 18 – Marriage / Family

Perspective

A Godly spouse is a gift from God. Foundations to a Godly marriage are: love, humility, truth, communication and empathy. By placing Christ first in your life, you are transformed to think, speak and act like Christ. You will be a better spouse, better parent, better child and better friend when you look to Jesus every day.

Proverbs 19:14

Fathers can give their sons an inheritance of houses and wealth, but only the LORD can give an understanding wife.

Hebrews 13:4-6

Give honor to marriage, and remain faithful to one another in marriage. God will surely judge people who are immoral and those who commit adultery. Don't love money; be satisfied with what you have. For God has said, "I will never fail you. I will never abandon you. So we can say with confidence, "The LORD is my helper, so I will have no fear. What can mere people do to me?"

Proverbs 5:15

Drink water from your own well— share your love only with your wife.

Please Pray Before You Begin

Date:_____

My Key Verses For: Marriage / Family

_____

_____

_____

_____

_____

_____

_____

My Perspective

_____

_____

_____

_____

_____

_____

_____

_____

_____

Please Pray Before You Begin

Date:_____

My Key Verses For: Marriage / Family

_____

_____

_____

_____

_____

_____

My Perspective

_____

_____

_____

_____

_____

_____

_____

_____

**"Surround yourself with people
who see your strengths."**

- James S Foubister IV

Day 19 – Missions

Perspective

God has deputized you to share the good news of salvation with every nation. Invest your time and heart with others, creating disciples who will go and share. How will they hear if no one is sent? **"Tell"** others about Jesus in your life is the #1 word in the NLT Bible! **"Tell"** appears six hundred and forty one times in the New Living Translation (NLT) Bible!

Romans 10:14-15

But how can they call on him to save them unless they believe in him? And how can they believe in him if they have never heard about him? And how can they hear about him unless someone tells them? And how will anyone go and tell them without being sent? That is why the Scriptures say, "How beautiful are the feet of messengers who bring good news!"

Isaiah 52:7

How beautiful on the mountains are the feet of the messenger who brings good news, the good news of peace and salvation, the news that the God of Israel reigns!

Please Pray Before You Begin

Date:_____

My Key Verses For: Missions

_____

_____

_____

_____

_____

_____

_____

My Perspective

_____

_____

_____

_____

_____

_____

_____

_____

_____

Please Pray Before You Begin

Date:_____

My Key Verses For: Missions

_____

_____

_____

_____

_____

_____

_____

_____

My Perspective

_____

_____

_____

_____

_____

_____

_____

_____

'The church is a refuge for the world, not a refuge from the world."

- James Foubister V

Day 20 – Motives / Truth

Perspective

It is important you understand that God knows YOUR motives. Our heart is reflected in what we say. Our motives are evident in our deeds and purpose. Your pride will be a poison to pure motives. Do not let pride scar your heart or damage your mind. Remember God will shine His light on your darkest secrets. You will be judged by every idle word you speak.

Proverbs 16:2

People may be pure in their own eyes, but the LORD examines their motives.

1 Corinthians 4:5

My conscience is clear, but that doesn't prove I'm right. It is the Lord himself who will examine me and decide.

Matthew 12:36

And I tell you this, you must give an account on judgment day for every idle word you speak.

John 14:6

Jesus told him, "I am the way, the truth, and the life. No one can come to the Father except through me.

John 8:32

And you will know the truth, and the truth will set you free

Please Pray Before You Begin

Date:_____

My Key Verses For: Motives / Truth

_____

_____

_____

_____

_____

_____

_____

My Perspective

_____

_____

_____

_____

_____

_____

_____

_____

Please Pray Before You Begin

Date:_____

My Key Verses For: Motives / Truth

_____
_____
_____
_____
_____
_____
_____

My Perspective

_____
_____
_____
_____
_____
_____
_____
_____
_____

"In God's name, stop a moment, cease your work, look around you!"

-Leo Tolstoy

Day 21 – Pastors

Perspective

Pastors' have God's authority to teach and live the bible. They make disciples by feeding their flock. You help your Pastor so they can spend more time with God. If you are a leader, your priority is to help your pastor. Today, ask your pastor how you can help!

Hebrews 13:7

Remember your leaders who taught you the word of God. Think of all the good that has come from their lives, and follow the example of their faith.

Hebrews 13:17

Obey your spiritual leaders, and do what they say. Their work is to watch over your souls, and they are accountable to God. Give them reason to do this with joy and not with sorrow. That would certainly not be for your benefit.

Ephesians 4:12-13

Their responsibility is to equip God's people to do his work and build up the church, the body of Christ. This will continue until we all come to such unity in our faith and knowledge of God's Son that we will be mature in the Lord, measuring up to the full and complete standard of Christ.

Please Pray Before You Begin

Date:_____

My Key Verses For Pastors

_____

_____

_____

_____

_____

_____

_____

My Perspective

_____

_____

_____

_____

_____

_____

_____

_____

Please Pray Before You Begin

Date:_____

My Key Verses For: Pastors

_____

_____

_____

_____

_____

_____

_____

_____

My Perspective

_____

_____

_____

_____

_____

_____

_____

_____

_____

"Pure religion in the eyes of God is one that helps widows and orphans in distress, and not let the world corrupt you."

-James the brother of Jesus

Day 22 – Eternity

Perspective

God cannot lie, He is 100% truth. He promises a life in eternity with Him, to everyone (you) who loves him with all their heart, mind and soul. Think, live and share your Jesus with others. This will show you love your neighbor as yourself. If you do this, you will live forever in heaven with Jesus!

Ecclesiastes 3:11

Yet God made everything beautiful for it's own time. He has planted eternity into the human heart, but even so, people cannot see the whole scope of God's work from beginning to the end.

John 3:15-16

So that everyone who believes in him will have eternal life. For God loved the world so much that he gave his one and only Son, so that everyone who believes in will not perish but have eternal life.

John 5:24

I tell you the truth, those who listen to my message and believe in God who sent me have eternal life. They will never be condemned for their sims, but they have already passed from death to life.

Revelation 22:12

Look I am coming soon, bringing my reward with me to repay all people according to their deeds.

Please Pray Before You Begin

Date:_____

My Key Verses For Eternity

_____

_____

_____

_____

_____

_____

_____

_____

My Perspective

_____

_____

_____

_____

_____

_____

_____

_____

_____

Please Pray Before You Begin

Date:_____

My Key Verses For: Eternity

_____

_____

_____

_____

_____

_____

_____

My Perspective

_____

_____

_____

_____

_____

_____

_____

_____

_____

"Look to where God is working, then go and help."

-Dr. Henry Blackaby

Day 23 – Priorities

Perspective

T3 = Time, treasure and talent. Where we spend our time shows our love of Christ. Where we spend our money, shows our love of Christ. When you help others with your talent, this shows your love of Christ. Try and keep these as your priorities.

Store your treasures in Heaven.

Matthew 10:32-33

"Everyone who acknowledges me publicly here on earth, I will also acknowledge before my Father in heaven But everyone who denies me here on earth, I will also deny before my Father in heaven

Matthew 6:33

Seek the Kingdom of God above all else, and live righteously, and he will give you everything you need.

Romans 12:2

Don't copy the behavior and customs of this world, but let God transform you into a new person by changing the way you think. Then you will learn to know God's will for you, which is good and pleasing and perfect.

Please Pray Before You Begin

Date:_____

My Key Verses For: Priorities

_____

_____

_____

_____

_____

_____

_____

My Perspective

_____

_____

_____

_____

_____

_____

_____

_____

_____

Please Pray Before You Begin

Date:_____

My Key Verses For: Priorities

_____

_____

_____

_____

_____

_____

_____

My Perspective

_____

_____

_____

_____

_____

_____

_____

_____

"God blesses those who are merciful, for they will be shown Mercy"

-Jesus Christ

Day 24 – Purpose for Christ

Perspective

Doing God's will in your life is your purpose. You are called to make disciples of Jesus. You are called to reconcile others to God. God has you on a path He has prepared. Do not lean on your own understanding. Trust God in everything you do! "Loving Others" with the comfort of Jesus Christ is one of your purposes.

Romans 8:28-29

And we know that God causes everything to work together for the good of those who love God and are called according to his purpose for them. For God knew his people in advance, and he chose them to become like his Son, so that his Son would be the firstborn among many brothers and sisters.

1 Corinthians 9:26-27

So I run with purpose in every step. I am not just shadowboxing. I discipline my body like an athlete, training it to do what it should. Otherwise, I fear that after preaching to others I myself might be disqualified.

Proverbs 19:21

You can make many plans, but the LORD'S purpose will prevail.

Please Pray Before You Begin

Date:_____

My Key Verses For: Purpose For Christ

_____

_____

_____

_____

_____

_____

_____

_____

My Perspective

_____

_____

_____

_____

_____

_____

_____

_____

_____

Please Pray Before You Begin

Date:_____

My Key Verses For: Purpose For Christ

_____

_____

_____

_____

_____

_____

_____

My Perspective

_____

_____

_____

_____

_____

_____

_____

_____

"When we speak the truth with love, we are Jesus Christ's best weapon against sin.

-James S Foubister IV

Day 25 – Reading Scripture

Perspective

Reading the bible is the source of wisdom and discernment. Reading, studying and memorizing scripture gives you the foundation for peace, love and faith in your life. The word of God is the fuel for your Holy Spirit. Consider a daily devotional with the bible to keep you in God's will!

Your best protection from Satan is memorized bible verses.

Joshua 1:8-9

Study this Book of Instruction continually. Meditate on it day and night so you will be sure to obey everything written in it. Only then will you prosper and succeed in all you do. This is my command—be strong and courageous! Do not be afraid or discouraged. For the LORD your God is with you wherever you go."

Ezra 7:10

This was because Ezra had determined to study and obey the Law of the LORD and to teach those decrees and regulations to the people of Israel.

Mark 4:11

He replied, "You are permitted to understand the secret of the Kingdom of God. But I use parables for everything I say to outsiders.

Please Pray Before You Begin

Date:_____

My Key Verses For: Reading Scripture

_____
_____
_____
_____
_____
_____
_____

My Perspective

_____
_____
_____
_____
_____
_____
_____
_____
_____

Please Pray Before You Begin

Date:_____

My Key Verses For: Reading Scripture

_____
_____
_____
_____
_____
_____
_____

My Perspective

_____
_____
_____
_____
_____
_____
_____
_____
_____

"If you judge people, you have no time to love them."

-Mother Teresa

Day 26 – Salvation

Perspective

God chooses you! His prevenient grace is seen in His pursuit of you. You cannot earn salvation through good deeds or donation. Salvation is God's gift to you. When you confess with your mouth, Jesus is Lord, and believe in your heart that he was raised from the dead, you are **saved**. Jesus prepaid to God your debt for your repented sin. Jesus promises to send and advocate, a helper, in the form of the Holy Spirit, to all who accept Christ.

Romans 11:11

Did God's people stumble and fall beyond recovery? Of course not! They were disobedient, so God made salvation available to the Gentiles. But he wanted his own people to become jealous and claim it for themselves.

2 Corinthians 5:17-18

This means that anyone who belongs to Christ has become a new person. The old life is gone; a new life has begun! And all of this is a gift from God, who brought us back to himself through Christ. And God has given us this task of reconciling people to him.

1 Timothy 2:5-6

For there is only one God and one mediator who can reconcile God and humanity-that is the man Christ Jesus. He gave his life to purchase freedom for everyone.This is the message God gave to the world at just the right time.

Please Pray Before You Begin

Date:_____

My Key Verses For: Salvation

_____

_____

_____

_____

_____

_____

_____

_____

My Perspective

_____

_____

_____

_____

_____

_____

_____

_____

Please Pray Before You Begin

Date:_____

My Key Verses For: Salvation

_____

_____

_____

_____

_____

_____

My Perspective

_____

_____

_____

_____

_____

_____

_____

_____

"Show me a man whose bible is falling apart, and I will show you a man who is not."

- Doc Malwin

Day 27 – Serving Others

Perspective

Jesus commands us to "Love Others". In today's practical terms, it is to say, "How can I help you". Service is not a duty but rather a gift you are giving to GOD. You are to help the poor, the disabled, the hurting, the disadvantaged, by doing so, you are following the great command Jesus gave us, "Love your neighbor as I have loved you."

.

Galatians 6:10

Therefore, whenever we have the opportunity, we should do good to everyone—especially to those in the family of faith.

James 2:24

So you see, we are shown to be right with God by what we do, not by faith alone.

Matthew 5:16

In the same way, let your good deeds shine out for all to see, so that everyone will praise your heavenly Father.

John 13:3-5

So he got up from the table, took off his robe, wrapped a towel around his waist, and poured water into a basin. Then he began to wash the disciples' feet, drying them with the towel he had around him.

Hebrews 10:24

Let us think of ways to motivate one another to acts of love and good works.

Please Pray Before You Begin

Date:_____

My Key Verses For: Serving Others

_____

_____

_____

_____

_____

_____

_____

My Perspective

_____

_____

_____

_____

_____

_____

_____

_____

_____

Please Pray Before You Begin

Date:_____

My Key Verses For: Serving Others

_____

_____

_____

_____

_____

_____

_____

My Perspective

_____

_____

_____

_____

_____

_____

_____

_____

"God's love never let's go, and HIS face never turns away."

-Dr. David Allen

Day 28 – Sin

Perspective

The potential of us sinning is present every day. Sin is always in our minds. Our minds are distracted every hour or minute by thoughts of pride, entitlement, possessions, lust, envy and the love of money. All temptations start in our mind. Your Holy Spirit, fed with scripture and prayer, will extinguish all temptation. God offers his followers grace and forgiveness for all REPENTED sin. Your repentance gives you a clean beginning with God every day.

1 John 2:1-2

My dear children, I am writing this to you so that you will not sin. But if anyone does sin, we have an advocate who pleads our case before the Father. He is Jesus Christ, the one who is truly righteous. He himself is the sacrifice that atones for our sins—and not only our sins but the sins of all the world.

James 4:17

Remember, it is sin to know what you ought to do and then not do it.

John 8:24

That is why I said that you will die in your sins: for unless you believe that I Am who I claim to be you will die in your sins.

John 16:9

The world's sin is that it refuses to believe in me.

Romans 6:23

For the wages of sin is death, but the free gift of God is eternal life through Christ Jesus our Lord.

Please Pray Before You Begin

Date: _____

My Key Verses For: Sin

_____

_____

_____

_____

_____

_____

_____

My Perspective

_____

_____

_____

_____

_____

_____

_____

_____

Please Pray Before You Begin

Date: _____

My Key Verses For: Sin

_____

_____

_____

_____

_____

_____

_____

My Perspective

_____

_____

_____

_____

_____

_____

_____

_____

"You are God's partner, made in the image of God and paid for at a great cost"

-James Foubister V

Day 29 – Trinity

Perspective

GOD is the father who created the world and all things in it. He chose to make Adam to be his friend and then he made Eve so Adam would have a companion. GOD saw humanity living in sin and making up laws and rules to promote themselves. GOD'S covenant in the Old Testament was harsh with many consequences to disobey his commands and teaching. He saw a need in humanity for a way to redeem the sinful nature we humans have. His second covenant of the blood of Jesus Christ, His only begotten SON, was our redemption of sin. Jesus paid for all our repented sin. As Jesus did this, he embarked on a humanity charged with "Loving Others as Jesus loves us."

This gift of salvation GOD gave us can only be accepted when we "Confess with your mouth Jesus is Lord and believe in your heart he was raised from the dead." It is at that moment we are saved and will live in the Kingdom of GOD forever. He sent us a helper and advocate at the moment we are saved. This Holy Spirit is our helper and advocate.

John 14:15-21

"If you love me, obey my commandments. And I will ask the Father, and he will give you another Advocate who will never leave you. He is the Holy Spirit, who leads into all truth. The world cannot receive him, because it isn't looking for him and doesn't recognize him. But you know him, because he lives with you now and later will be in you.

No, I will not abandon you as orphans—I will come to you. Soon the world will no longer see me, but you will see me. Since I live, you also will live.

When I am raised to life again, you will know that I am in my Father, and you are in me, and I am in you. Those who accept my commandments and obey them are the ones who love me. And because they love me, my Father will love them. And I will love them and reveal myself to each of them."

John 15:26

"But I will send you the Advocate—the Spirit of truth. He will come to you from the Father and will testify all about me.

John 16:7-8

But in fact, it is best for you that I go away, because if I don't, the Advocate won't come. If I do go away, then I will send him to you. And when he comes, he will convict the world of its sin, and of God's righteousness, and of the coming judgment.

Please Pray Before You Begin

Date:_____

My Key Verses For: Trinity

_____

_____

_____

_____

_____

_____

_____

My Perspective

_____

_____

_____

_____

_____

_____

_____

_____

Please Pray Before You Begin

Date:_____

My Key Verses For: Trinity

_____

_____

_____

_____

_____

_____

_____

My Perspective

_____

_____

_____

_____

_____

_____

_____

_____

"Do your little bit of good where you are; it's those little bits of good put together that overwhelm the world."

-Desmond Tutu

Day 30 – Unity In Church/Unity With Others

Perspective

Unity is a gift GOD gives you when you are living GOD'S way in your mind, heart and soul. Then, you will see the good in others. You will have a pure heart and see the commonness of Jesus which binds us together. Unity is the key ingredient to peace in your life. You must be an example of unity. Love for others is the engine of unity.

John 17:20-23

I am praying not only for these disciples but also for all who will ever believe in me through their message. I pray that they will all be one, just as you and I are one—as you are in me, Father, and I am in you. And may they be in us so that the world will believe you sent me. I have given them the glory you gave me, so they may be one as we are one. I am in them and you are in me. May they experience such perfect unity that the world will know that you sent me and that you love them as much as you love me.

Philippians 2:2-5

Then make me truly happy by agreeing wholeheartedly with each other, loving one another, and working together with one mind and purpose. Don't be selfish; don't try to impress others. Be humble, thinking of others as better than yourselves Don't look out only for your own interests, but take an interest in others, too. You must have the same attitude that Christ Jesus had.

Please Pray Before You Begin

Date: _____

My Key Verses For: Unity In Church / Unity With Others

_____

_____

_____

_____

_____

_____

_____

_____

My Perspective

_____

_____

_____

_____

_____

_____

_____

_____

_____

Please Pray Before You Begin

Date: _____

My Key Verses For: Unity In Church/Unity With Others

_____
_____
_____
_____
_____
_____
_____
_____

My Perspective

_____
_____
_____
_____
_____
_____
_____
_____
_____
_____

"When all are in UNITY, there lies HEAVEN"

-James Foubister IV

Day31 -Wisdom

Perspective

Wisdom is more valuable than gold, more precious than silver and is your gift to others. It is pure truth spoken with love. It fuels patience, essential to loving others. It protects your tongue so you will encourage others with your spoken words. It gives you the gift of empathy and a character of integrity.

James 3:17-18

But the wisdom from above is first of all pure. It is also peace loving, gentle at all times, and willing to yield to others. It is full of mercy and good deeds. It shows no favoritism and is always sincere. And those who are peacemakers will plant seeds of peace and reap a harvest of righteousness.

Proverbs 4:4-7

My father taught me, Take my words to heart. Follow my commands, and you will live. Get wisdom; develop good judgment. Don't forget my words or turn away from them. Don't turn your back on wisdom, for she will protect you. Love her, and she will guard you. Getting wisdom is the wisest thing you can do! And whatever else you do, develop good judgment If you prize wisdom, she will make you great. Embrace her, and she will honor you.

Please Pray Before You Begin

Date:_____

My Key Verses For: Wisdom

_____

_____

_____

_____

_____

_____

_____

My Perspective

_____

_____

_____

_____

_____

_____

_____

_____

_____

Please Pray Before You Begin

Date:_____

My Key Verses For: Wisdom

_____

_____

_____

_____

_____

_____

_____

My Perspective

_____

_____

_____

_____

_____

_____

_____

_____

Notes

His Burden Is Light

Lord I pray I gratefully take your yolk upon me!

For you promise it is easy to bear!

The burden you give me is to know you better!

Lord I pray that I know you better, through my prayers!

Lord I pray that I know you better, through reading your word!

Lord I pray that I know you better, through my acts of kindness!

Lord I pray that I know you better, through inviting someone to Church!

Lord I pray that I know you better, through sharing my testimony with others!

Lord I pray that I know you better, through encouraging others in following you!

Lord I pray you know me better as I live out my faith with you!

Day 32 - Your Day

Perspective

You are at the end of an incredible journey. Your first draft of your devotional.

Congratulations on practicing daily prayer, reading daily scripture and daily reflection. My wish for you is to continue to share your walk with Christ!

Well Done Good And Faithful Servant

Your spiritual heritage, that you have prepared for your future generations, is now a reality with Legacy 31. Your heart, mind, motives, faith, hope and love has been transcribed to glorify God to others.

Legacy 31 is found at the intersection of faith, hope and love. Here you felt God's mercy, love and grace which He has poured into your life. You have likely noticed that Legacy 31 has no net worth information, no career section, no salaries, no degrees, no achievement section, no position held, no recognition and no accomplishment.

It only shares your love of Jesus Christ. Because no matter where your future generations are in life, rich or poor, healthy or sick, free or enslaved, a life with Christ can be theirs.

No matter what has been their past, God gives us new mercies every day. They can say to God, "use me today Lord for your purpose."

It is important you embrace this pure communication of your love of Christ you have shared.

As you embrace your love for Christ you will move closer to being content with your life, and live happily with much or with little. The cornerstone for contentment is doing His work in your life. If it is to pray then pray. If it is to teach his word then teach. If it is to help others then serve, if it is to spend time with the needy then visit. Do not be confused, contentment is not being comfortable. Contentment is accepting all God has provided you, your time, treasures and talent and showing the love of Christ by using those generously for others.

You are likely closer to God today, the day you finished your first draft of Legacy 31, than any other time in your life. You have studied His word. Listened to him through your Holy Spirit, as you shared your perspective each day. You did not ask others for what verse sounded correct because whatever the Lord led you to share is correct. You did not compete with anyone. This was not a race of any kind. It was all about YOU and your love of Jesus.

Be ready now, your heart has been purified. As Jesus shared in Matthew 5:8, **"Blessed are those with a pure heart for they will see God"**. As you see God look carefully because He wants to hand you His gift of contentment because He sees you as His great friend.

In His Service

Your Friend in Jesus Christ

James S. Foubister IV

Made in the USA
Columbia, SC
11 October 2024

43433585R00100